BASICS OF PROPERTY AND FACILITIES MANAGEMENT

ANOOP KHANDEKAR

ISBN
Hardcase 979-8-89961-252-7
Paperback 979-8-89498-378-3

Dedicated To

"I dedicate this book to

–   My Wife Harshada who made sure I do not lose sight of my purpose and Completed this book conquering all Odds

–   My Lovely Daughters Sarayu and Soumya who delightfully offered to play the role of Guinea Pigs for my Pilot Management Projects at Home and continue to be Inspiring source of my Evergreen Creative Energy"

Contents

PART 2

Basics of Property Management in the Indian Context

Foreword

It is with great admiration and joy that I present this insightful guide on Facilities Management, penned with dedication during a time of global pause and reflection. The lockdown was a catalyst for my dear friend and mentor, Anoop, turning a challenging period into an opportunity to share invaluable knowledge.

Facilities Management professionals are the unsung heroes and the backbone of efficiency and progress of any organization. This book serves as an essential guide not only for those entering this dynamic domain, it also offers practical insights and actionable knowledge for each of us, known as **FMiets**.

What sets this work apart is its clarity and focus, reflecting Anoop's deep understanding of the subject and a genuine desire to empower others. This book is relatable and a companion in navigating the complexities of the FM Industry. Whether it is to do with budget constraints, client approvals, reliance on manual skill, adoption of technology, tiding over the pandemic-like situation, delayed payments, low margins, or a constant requirement of delivering innovation and efficiency.

It is a privilege to contribute these words to the efforts, love and expertise. May this guide inspire confidence, curiosity, and competence in every FM professional.

Sincerely,

– Sitanshu Shekhar Singhdeo
VP - FM
Brigade Group

PART 1

Basics of Facilities Management in the Indian Context

Overview

The Facilities Management Industry, which came to India around 1998, is one of the fastest-growing services. Yet, it remains quite nascent and underdeveloped in terms of the quality of resources and services vis-a-vis client expectations.

There are multiple reasons, ranging from budget constraints, Non-Standard Management systems, and practices which rely heavily on manual skill rather than technology, to the availability of training facilities and faculties. We have reasons to believe that it is a matter of will rather than skill for the industry to invest in the required time and resources for training and retraining of staff at various levels and to maintain continuity of improvement in Human Skill index required for the desired output.

Most of the people working in this industry come from varied academic and social backgrounds as this industry is very flexible to adapt to differently qualified and experienced people, enabling them to gel and absorb seamlessly to cater to fast-paced requirements. However, a low entry barrier has become a major challenge for organisations operating in this field to attract, groom, and retain talent.

This book aims to partially fill this gap and assist all the career aspirants in this industry who wish to grow in their career by understanding the industry basics and to build upon them in their respective workspaces.

We have a firm belief that readers will use this opportunity to renew their vigour and enhance potential by building on the basics covered here.

Definition & Importance of F.M

Definitions

Facilities Management can be defined as managing the premises, work environment, and non-core business support services for the clients.

Integrated Facilities Management - This includes consolidated provision of hard and soft services, as well as management of general support and specialist maintenance services.

Facility Management essentially combines **people**, **Processes**, and **technology** to deliver its services to client, thereby increasing asset **Productivity** and **Profitability**, using expertise to save cost.

Any workspace - be it a commercial office premises, factory, hotel, or mall - needs to be maintained with proper cleaning, technical maintenance, and assisting the clients/owners to enhance their respective customer experience, to delight them, and thereby retain them and attract more customers.

The main objective of the Facility Maintenance department of any organisation is:

- Enhance Asset's Life.
- Maintaining premises in a state-of-the-art condition to deliver customer delight.
- Save valuable time for the client so that they can focus on their core business.
- Optimise the maintenance costs through continuous improvement and innovation.

F.M, therefore, has become a very important aspect of the Real Estate Industry in modern times, and with continuous enhancement in real estate product quality, the demand and expertise are expected to grow exponentially.

India FM Market and Growth Scenario

Indian FM industry market is expected to be above 150 billion USD by 2025. Its growth rate is anticipated to be 14-20% year-on-year, which makes it a very important and attractive sector for growth. According to the report, 75% of the Indian market is still untapped for FM.

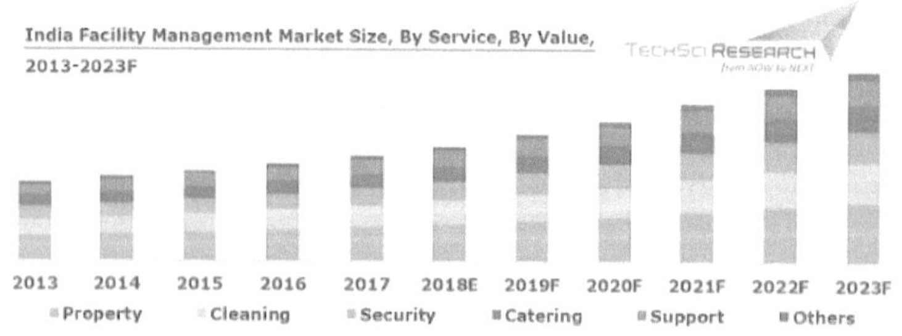

This makes it ideal in the service industry to focus on employment and skill development.

Outsourcing, Subject Matter Expertise, and Value Proposition

Since Facilities Management is a non-core activity for the clients, it is outsourced to a Professional FM Services company, also known as an **FM Service Provider (FMSP).** These FMSPs are experts in their field of operations and can make their expertise available as required to the client at reasonable, competitive costs. So, as a principal, outsourcing to FMSPs is the trend in the FM industry, which is preferred worldwide.

Major FMSPs in India are as follows:

C. B. Richard Ellis Ltd (CBRE)

Jones Lang LaSalle (JLL)

Sodexho

Cushman & Wakefield

Knight Frank India Ltd.

BVG India Ltd

Updater Services

Tenon Ltd

ISS Ltd

QUESS (AVON)

03

Hard Services

These are mainly Technical Services like Provision of Qualified and Trained manpower for Operation & Maintenance (O&M), along with necessary tools and tackles as required. Major ones are as listed below:

Mechanical and Electrical Maintenance

Provision of qualified and trained manpower for operating and maintaining building infrastructure like electrical installation-HT/LT substation and power & lighting distribution. This also includes power backup systems such as diesel generators, UPS, inverters, and solar panels. Mechanical systems include pumps, chiller plants, Air conditioning systems, compressors, etc.

Plumbing, Water Supply, and Drainage/Sewage System

This includes Operation & Maintenance of water supply, storage and sewage handling and drainage infrastructure via Sewage Treatment Plant (STP) and Water Treatment Plant (WTP).

Civil structure maintenance

This includes maintaining building elevation-facade, painting and timely Structural Certification throughout the life of a building. Civil structure maintenance can also include structure strengthening works, upgradation of interior works.

Precision and Comfort Air Conditioning System

This covers Special Cooling Infrastructure for Data Centres and Computer Rooms

Fire safety systems - Hydrants, Sprinklers, VESDA (Very Early Smoke Detection Apparatus), Alarm Systems.

This Includes Fire Detection and Fire Fighting equipment maintenance, certification and testing.

Lighting and Electrical Power Distribution Systems.

Security System: CCTV, Access Control, Boom Barriers.

Building Management System (BMS)

Lifts, Elevators, and Escalators

Services Delivery Methodology

Any client requiring the provision of outsourcing the hard services for its facility issues a "Request for Proposal" or RFP to the interested FM Service Providers or MEPC (Marine Environmental Protection Committee) contractors. The client may also ask Project Management or Installation of Systems companies to quote for hard services when starting a new facility. An RFP contains a brief overview of:

- The Make, Quantity, Type, and Specifications of all MEPC installations as mentioned above in Hard Services.
- List of all Assets with warranty details.
- Operating Hours and specific manpower requirements (Qualification/Experience, etc.)
- Type of Maintenance required: Comprehensive and Non-Comprehensive.
- Quality of Outputs or Service levels expected are also specified.

Usually, a site visit is also organised for interested parties, where they are expected to conduct a detailed survey and ask questions for a better understanding of client requirements, and to determine the manpower, materials, and tools required to perform the activities for the desired client output.

All Proposals and Costs are then requested and sought by the client in a typical format. Usually, the proposals are sought for manpower costs plus the profit percentage of the cost for the materials used. The proposals are for monthly manpower deployed costs for a minimum 12-month contract period, extendable up to many more years.

Service Delivery Procedure

1. Manpower Structure is finalised along with respective Job Descriptions (JDs) and its deployed at site after proper selection by relevant client authorities.

Asset List and Preventive Maintenance Schedule (PPM) are finalised and approved.

2. Operations Budget (Opex) and Capex budgets are approved.
3. Tools, Spares, and Consumables Ordered and Stocked
4. Checklists, logbooks, and history cards for all equipment are made.
5. Standard Operating Procedures (SOPs)s, safety documents like risk assessment, and work permits are made available on the ground.
6. Basic Induction and training to all Staff and Vendors.
7. Outsourced Services Contracts for specialised assets such as Lifts, Chillers ETC are Issued to respective Original Equipment Manufacturers (OEM's) and Standard Service Levels (SLAs) are agreed and implemented.
8. Daily/Weekly/Monthly reports of Corrective and Preventive maintenance are maintained on Computerised Facility Management System (CAFM) or manually as per the contract.
9. Asset and Service Health Status is reported daily, weekly and monthly in reports such as Monthly Management Report (MMR) and Reviewed.
10. Regular Service/Tool/Quality, and Safety Audits are carried out as per client calendar or SOP.

04

Soft Services

These are mainly non-technical services listed as below.

- Cleaning Services: Mainly housekeeping services
- Waste Management
- Horticulture
- Pest Control
- Security and Guarding
- Pantry and Cafeteria Services Management.

These are usually manpower based services and service output driven services.

Service Delivery Methodology

Here, the client usually floats an RFP, followed by a site survey visit to understand the scope of services and then works out the manpower, tools, and material requirements for the desired level of output.

All Proposals and Costs are then requested and sought by the client in a typical format. Usually, the proposals are sought for a manpower cost-plus basis. The proposals are per month manpower deployed costs for a period of a minimum 12-month contract period, up to many more years' extendable contract.

Service Delivery Procedure

The Procedure for Service Delivery is similar to hard services. A summary, for easy understanding, is as follows:

Service	Scope of Work	Daily	Weekly	Fortnightly	Monthly	Quarterly	Half Yearly	Annual	MIS	Monitoring Measure
Cleaning	√			Activity/Deliverable SLA					Available	Performance Control
Waste Management	√			Activity/Deliverable SLA					Available	Performance Control
Horticulture	√			Activity/Deliverable SLA					Available	Performance Control
Pest Control	√			Activity/Deliverable SLA					Available	Performance Control
Security & Guarding	√			Activity/Deliverable SLA					Available	Performance Control
Pantry Sevices	√			Activity/Deliverable SLA					Available	Performance Control
Cafetaria Management	√			Activity/Deliverable SLA					Available	Performance Control

1. Manpower Structure is finalised along with respective Job Descriptions (JDs) and its deployed at site after proper selection by relevant Client Authorities.
2. Area Cleaning Schedules (PPM) are finalised and approved for different cleaning requirements such as hard floor/carpet etc.
3. Operations Budget (Opex) and Capex budgets are approved.
4. Tools, Spares, and Consumables Ordered and Stocked
5. Checklists, logbooks, and history cards for all equipment are made.

6. Standard Operating Procedures (SOPs)s, safety documents like risk assessment, and work permits are made available on the ground.
7. Basic Induction and training to all Staff and Vendors.
8. Outsourced Services Contracts for specialised services such as Carpet Shampooing, Glass Cleaning, etc.are finalised with Specialist Suppliers and SLAs agreed and implemented.
9. Daily/Weekly/Monthly reports of Corrective and Preventive maintenance are maintained on Computerised Facility Management System (CAFM) or manually as per the contract.
10. Cleaning Status is reported in MMR and Reviewed.
11. Regular Service/Tool/Quality, and Safety Audits are Carried out in-house or third party as per client SOP.

General Admin Support Services

These are the office support services that most clients nowadays prefer to outsource to minimise their on-roll staff requirement, giving them flexibility and reducing overhead costs. The main aim is to increase the output of these services without creating a liability for the client organisation. Typical admin support services are as follows:

- Reception and front desk.
- Event Management.
- Reprographic stations (printers/xerox machine etc.) management.
- Stationery and Office supplies management,
- Helpdesk-Offering a Single Point of Contact Cell Centre for users to report issue or request service
- Documents and records management includes offsite and on site storage of important documents.
- Asset, furniture and fixture management.

As a general guideline, the following are important points which are considered:

1. A Sound Policy is set for all above services, well defined and communicated to all users.
2. In case of software-based management, proper training and a back-end contract with the supplier is ensured.
3. Proper Storage Place - Online and Offline Storage Space is made available directly or through third party specialised record management company.
4. Procurement and Billing Interfaces are clearly understood and communicated to all team.
5. Proper job descriptions are created, and training at regular intervals is defined in Training Policy
6. Any Affiliation to Special Requirements such as ISO/British Standards (BSC) etc. is specified and services are supposed to cater for them.

Specialist Services

These are the specialised systems related maintenance services which may require an expert to maintain them. However, usually, these services are designed to be maintained by periodic inspections and, as and when required, visits by the Original Equipment Manufacturers' representative only, who is authorised to carry out the maintenance jobs. The operations of these systems can be done by the regular on-site maintenance team, but they have to be trained by the OEM representative on a regular basis. Following is a list of such services or systems, which is indicative only.

- Audio-Visual Systems include high end conferencing systems and board room equipment.
- Facade cleaning and maintenance
- Fire systems maintenance
- Computer server-related special CRAC Aircon units
- UPS systems
- Building Management Systems
- Parking Management System

- Lifts, elevators, and escalators
- Security Systems, such as CCTV, Access Control, FAS
- Diesel Gensets
- Chillers
- Water pumping systems
- Space and move management
- Staff Transport Services: Pick up and drop
- Concierge and Travel Desk Management.

Cost-Plus or All-Inclusive option

Usually, all these costs are directly paid by the clients, and FMSP is supposed to only coordinate for service delivery. However, now in many cases, the client may ask for these services to be maintained and billed by FMSP. **However, as the assets here belong to the client, it is always recommended that these services are maintained and paid for directly by the client.**

Quality, Health & Safety

Quality, health, and safety, popularly known as QHSE, is the buzzword in this industry. International certifications in this field are the new normal now, be it residential or commercial property/facility. British Safety Council (BSC) and IMS (Integrated Management System) accreditations are a must now to demonstrate quality standards of construction and maintenance, which assures all users, occupants, buyers, etc. Therefore, QHSE has now become integral in PM/FM services and is an independent department governing the overall service standards.

The main objective in the QHSE field for any organisation is to clearly spell out the policy document and ensure that each staff and vendor working on its premises is aware of it. This awareness needs to be translated into training and knowledge to ensure that safety rules and guidelines are followed in all aspects of work at all times, and proper records are maintained for legal purposes in the future.

Important Deliverables of QHSE Policy Document

- Risk identification and Mitigation, Risk Register.
- First Aid Provision Maintenance
- Incidents, Near Misses, Accident Investigation, and Records
- Emergency Evacuation Plan and readiness
- Fire Safety Drill Calendar
- List of Fire Wardens
- Safety Jackets, Masks, Torches, etc., for Wardens
- Power Backup Parameters, Testing Procedures, and Dates.
- Statutory Compliances, Inspections, and Dates, Technical and Non-technical
- IAQ (Indoor Air Quality), and Water, Food Quality Test frequency.
- OSHA (Occupational Health and Safety) guidelines
- Site Safety Manual
- Work Permits, PTW, Working at height/confined spaces, Critical infrastructure.
- Accident Investigation, Reporting and Root Cause analysis.
- Continuous improvement and development and implementation of safety culture.

Safety is a vast field and usually the client has a direct representative to monitor service provider operations. Usually ISO/BSC Standards are followed by all Client Organisations which clearly spells out requirements for each outsourced service by all parties including audit requirements.

Compliances Management

All the services, whether technical or non-technical, are governed by Shops and Establishment, Minimum Wages, and other Labour acts. It is the responsibility of the client, as a principal employer, to ensure compliance.

Compliance Confirmation on behalf of the client is a key deliverable of FMSP and is part of the essence of the Contractual Agreement. Following are the most important compliances that must be maintained on-site at all times and can be inspected by a Labour inspector or competent authority at any time.

- Attendance and Wage Register for all contract staff at the site.
- Adherence to provisions of the Contract Labour Registration Act (CLRA), including, but not limited to, PF and ESIC challans, paid copies.
- In case of Transport management – Vehicle Compliances, Driver Compliances, and Tax Paid receipts.
- Test Certificates for Water Tanks, Foods, Air Quality, and D.S. Sets Returns.

- Annual Electrical, Fire and Lift Inspections by Statutory Authorities.
- Consent to Operate (CTO), PWD, and Municipality Inspections for sanitation and hygiene.
- Pest Control Records
- Penal Deduction records for SLA-related contracts
- Payment Certificates to all Contractors.
- Quarterly or Half yearly Inspections and Duty Filing for Diesel Gensets, Lifts , Fire Systems as per National Building Code and State By Laws.
- Facade Cleaning, Inspection, and Test Certificates
- Payment of Govt. Taxes and Duties, as applicable, such as Annual Fire and Lift Inspections, property Tax, etc.
- Quarterly or Half yearly Inspections and Duty Filing for Diesel Gensets, Lifts, Fire Systems, etc. as per National Building Code and State Bylaws.

Introduction to C.A.F.M

Computer-Aided Facilities Management (CAFM) is now a must in all FM Services Contracts. Usually, it means a specialised generic or specific software tool either provided by the client or within the FMSP scope, with the following essential features.

- A Complaint Management Module (CMMS) to record, track, and evaluate the customer service requests and generate MIS with accurate analysis on SLAs in each category of Service.
- A PPM module for tracking the effectiveness of preventive maintenance of assets.
- A Financial module to assist in capturing costs, expenses, and tracking the budget of various categories of services.
- Visitor Management System for Assisting security in safe access to premises for staff, vendors, and visitors.
- Parking management system for parking, management
- Time and Attendance monitoring,

- – Automated, QR code-based, and geo-fencing-based Quality of Services monitoring
- – MIS module for Daily, Weekly, Monthly, and other specific reports, as required by the Contract, along with the capability to store scanned service reports of Outsourced vendors or specialist suppliers.

This CAFM, i.e. the Computer-Aided facility Management, may be paid on actuals by the client or may be included in contract costs, depending on the contract and client requirements. Care has to be taken to include or cover its costs in the proposal by FMSP and should not be missed out by any chance. Usually, help desk executives are expected to manage the CAFM; however, access to different teams to different modules is given based on actual need.

A range of high-end to local software (like Maximo from IBM) are available in the market, and many clients and FMSPs have developed their own software.

However, CAFM is often the most poorly implemented across the FM industry due to ambiguity or lack of clarity, authority, cost, and bureaucratic delays between the client, FMSP, and vendors. It is, therefore, very important for all parties to understand the importance of its implementation and its non-implementation. Delay often leads to wasted time and efforts by all parties at all management levels,

affecting the quality of FM services and customer satisfaction.

App-based Mobility Solutions for technical teams checking the assets are also very common. However, such a requirement has to be studied in detail before any cost commitment is made or sought from any party as it is very costly to implement and does not have the flexibility for FMSP to absorb costs in case of poor implementation or failure.

End-To-End FM Contract Management Cycle

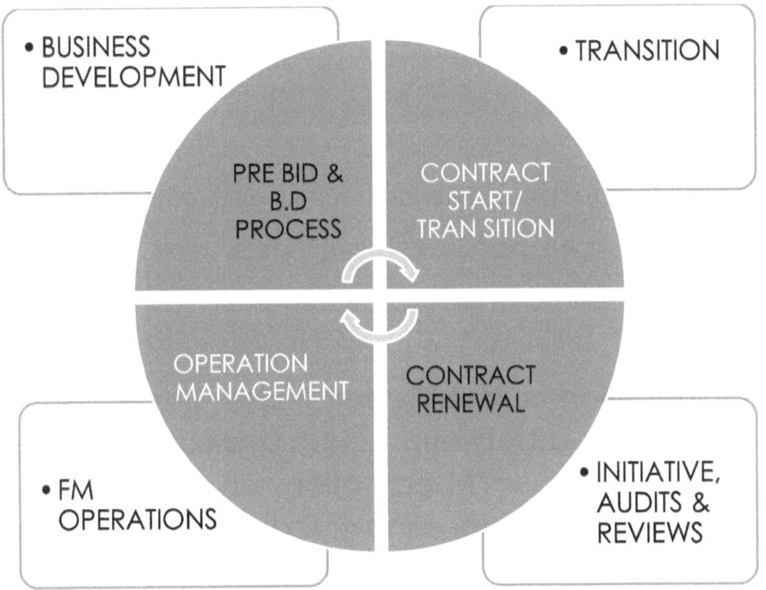

Business Development Stage This stage usually begins 30 to 90 days before a contract is intended to start from the Client. Usually, there are 3 stages of any new business development or Bid stage as illustrated below.

The first stage requires the client to prepare and circulate an RFP document, and organise visits and meetings for understanding the deliverables by the FMSP. The second stage consists of compiling proposals and evaluating the best service provider. The last stage is to award the contract.

Pre
- FLOATING OF RFP DOCUMENT TO VARIOUS FMSPs
- ORGANISING SITE VISITS AND PROVIDING THEM INFORMATION

Bid
- GETTING THE PROPOSALS FROM FMSPs
- ORGANISING PRESENTATION TO UNDERSTAND THE PROPOSAL
- EVALUATING COMPETENCY OF FMSP ON PROPOSAL AND ABILITY TO DELIVER SERVICES OF REQUIRED QUALITY

Post
- AWARD OF CONTRACT TO BEST QUALIFIED FMSP
- SIGNING OF CONTRACT AND COLLECTION OF RELEVANT BACK UP DOCUMENTS LIKE INSURANCES BG ETC

The Transition or Mobilisation Phase. The first 30 to 45-day period between contract awards and the startup of actual FM operations on the ground is referred to as the transition or mobilisation phase.

If the contract volume is large or consists of multiple sites or city operations, this phase may be billed extra and would require additional resources or a separate transition team to ensure that the entire contract setup is completed and operations start on the due date in time.

However, it is entirely a business decision between FMSP and client whether such services will be billed or included as value-added services from FMSP. Following are various types of transition requirements.

- Transition of a New Site – Takeover from Projects, set up of FM operations, and Handover to Operations team
- Transition from Outgoing FMSP and takeover and setup of FM operations.
- Transition from in-house team to outsourced FMSP team and set up of operations.
- Finding out gaps or snags in the facility and assigning the cost, priority, and responsibility to them is also a major activity of transition. **Basically, it means capturing damages and costs that existed before the contract started, and the client or outgoing FMSP should bear the rectification costs for these defects.**
- The transition team is an important link to understand the awarded contract with scope and Service level Agreements (SLAs). It has to transfer this to the operations team through training induction and briefing as a part of the contract startup deliverable and take sign-off internally to ensure compliance.

Transition is a very critical phase of any FM Contract, and the entire success or failure of the contract can be attributed to it. This is the reason why it is always preferable to have a separate Transition Team and Lead for every contract. The Transition team can be merged into the Operations team if required, providing flexibility to all parties. It is always advisable to form a skeletal transition team at the time of the Pre-Bid or Bid stage, and it should be involved right from the RFP stage and the preparation of the proposal. This approach comes in handy, saves time, and increases the effectiveness of contract implementation when the contract is awarded.

However, the ready availability of the Transition team on the bench is very unlikely with any FMSP due to cost constraints. A good FMSP can be distinguished from the rest based on the ability to cater to this requirement in a short time within its resources without compromising the quality of the Transition. Important objectives of transition can be outlined as below:

Finding out and rectification of the Snags in Facility

Recruitment, on-site Training, and Deployment of Operations team, and Outsourced Vendors along with uniform, Tools

Implementing control documentation such as Equipment Checklists

The expected SLA is above 95%, which will ensure the success of the contract accordingly.

FM Operations Stage the FMSP has to ensure that above 90% of committed resources for the Contract are available and deployed at Start date. Ideally, the on-site and on-job training, induction, and orientation have to be completed during the Transition phase; however, practically, this should be completed within 15 days of the Contract Start date. At the end of 35 days of the Contract Start date, the FMSP is supposed to submit separately the Transitions and Monthly Operations report to the Client capturing all the operations and contractual obligation details. Usually, the first monthly invoice and Transition Invoice are submitted along with the reports to the Client.

In addition to the delivery of standard agreed SLAs, as per the contract, an FMSP is supposed to carry out various internal audits as value-added services (Free of Cost) every quarter by engaging a Subject Matter Expert (SME) for services as listed below. The list is indicative and not exhaustive.

- Health and Safety Review
- Fire Evacuation Drills
- Soft Services Review
- Technical Audit
- Innovations and Process Improvements
- Cost Saving and Benchmarking Initiatives

Successful implementation of the above will ensure the renewal of the contract and the longevity of a healthy client relationship.

Quality of Service Delivery

Clients usually review the performance every month and on a quarterly basis at senior management levels based on MIS reports and achievement of SLAs. Often, SLAs are coupled with rewards and financial penalties or debits and serve as an indicator of the performance of FMSP over the contract period.

Contract Renewal Stage - This may be a repeat of the entire Bid Process or simply a commercial renegotiation depending on FMSP Performance and Client Requirements. In case the contract is not renewed or is lost, FMSP is required to **Demobilise** the site, which is kind of the reverse or opposite of mobilisation or Transition. Here, the FMSP has to close the operations and relocate its staff in accordance with the Contract and Client requirements.

Mis Reports and Important Checklists

Following are important MIS reports for any FM Contract.

A) Management Reports

- Daily Call Report
- Daily Operations Report
- Weekly Roster
- Weekly Operations review Tracker,
- Monthly Operations Report.
- Transition Report (Once at the Start of FM operations)
- Health & Safety Audit Review Report (Quarterly)
- Technical Services Review Report (Quarterly)
- Soft Services Audit Review Report (Quarterly)
- Statutory Compliance Report (Monthly)
- SLA Scorecard MIS (Monthly)
- Vendor performance report (Monthly)
- Customer Satisfaction Survey reports (Quarterly/ Half Yearly).
- Minutes of Meeting (All Important Meetings)

B) Financial Reports

- Annual Opex budget (due in contract month 1)
- Annual Capex Budget (due in contract month 3)
- Petty Cash Statement (monthly)
- Monthly Operation Cost Tracker
- Quarterly Operation Cost Review
- Annual Operating Cost Review
- Outstanding Payments Tracker (monthly)

FMSP usually carries out GOP analysis (Generally Operating Profit) Internally every quarter to ensure that Contract Profitability is maintained.

C) Technical Reports

- Daily Utilities Consumption Reports
- Spares & Consumables Monthly Report
- Asset Capacity Utilisation report (Monthly)
- Back up and redundancy report
- Asset Life Cycle Report (Quarterly)
- Critical Infrastructure Monthly Report.
- Space occupancy & Utilisation Monthly Report
- PPM – Planned vs Implemented Report
- D G Run Log
- D G Quarterly Returns Log
- Electrical Inspection Log,
- Lift Inspection Report
- Fire Inspection Report
- Pre-Monsoon Check Reports
- Leakages report.

- Structural Audit Report (Special)
- Technical Critical Asset Checklists (Daily/ Weekly/Monthly)
- Snag lists (as required)
- Facade Technical Inspection Report
- Municipality Inspection Report
- Power, Water, and Air Quality Report (Quarterly)
- Tank and Drain Cleaning Report (Hly)
- Earthling and Breakers Test Report (Annual)
- Fire Extinguisher Layout and Status Report

12

Cutomer Relationship Management (CRM)

CRM usually refers to the entire strategy and process of any FMSP to actively engage with clients at various levels with the purpose of increasing the effectiveness of communication, minimising dissatisfaction, and promptly identifying and acting on customer expectations to prolong the customer retention life cycle. FMSPs use multiple strategies and extensively incorporate technology for this purpose. There may be an independent vertical of CRM in an FMSP that interacts directly with clients and reports directly to senior management to remove undue influence or interference from operations team stakeholders of the contract.

Essentials of CRM

- There must be comprehensive spelled-out guidelines and a back-up budget with a detailed plan.
- CRM team leaders ideally should be carved out of various operations departments, and

     operatives should be on roles or third-party outsourced for effective implementation.

- Care must be taken to keep reports and findings confidential and closed by an independent authority, without any dependence on the operations team.
- Cohesive alliance is the responsibility of the Senior Management Team and should not be placed solely on the Operations team.
- CRM performance indicators should form important performance evaluation criteria for Bonus to the entire FMSP organisation. The penalty approach should be avoided.
- Use of software platform is highly advisable.
- Proper leader for CRM – selection is a must and should be a thorough profession in the field of FM.

Recommended Approach

- Extensive customer engagement activities every quarter.
- Software-based Complaint Module
- Scheduled meetings every month.
- Unscheduled calls and impromptu visits.

13

Essentials of a Good FMSP

An FMSP has to be strong financially and should be very effective in timely billing and collection. This helps in efficient supplier payments.

Also, a very strong supply chain of FMSP will help to get good leveraging and discounts with vendors, and improve profitability by exploiting the difference between sourcing and billed costs of service to the client.

Usually, the difference between a good and average FMSP is its staff retention and turnover. This has a cascading impact on customer contracts and FMSP profitability. A good system-based and professional regular training to staff and a robust engagement management policy at all levels will do the trick. At lower staff salary costs, better performance can be achieved. More reliance on CAFM should be done to increase productivity, and profitability will be taken care of.

All of the above will be useless if a strong central operations support team is not empowered, and unbiased review and reporting by Middle and Senior management teams is not followed. Ideally, staff should be treated above customers in importance as a philosophy, and it will do wonders.

It would be prudent to quote Mr Richard Branson, owner of Virgin Atlantic Airlines who had said, "Companies should put employees first and customers second to stay profitable and remain in business."

14

How to Be a Perfect FM Professional

A facility manager is supposed to be the best custodian for its client's property and assets, keeping it safe and operational 24/7/365 in the presence and absence of stakeholders. Therefore, it's very important for a good FM to be brutally integral and honest in its professional ethics, as any lapse will not only be a breach of contract but will also impact at three levels: the client, the self-organisation, and the vendor markets.

Often, contracts have loosely or too generically defined job descriptions for various roles in the FM team, which results in unequal work distribution, stresses, and conflicts in the team, leading to poor team output. All job descriptions should be specifically tailored for each contract, with specific outputs clearly defined and no overlap between any 2 positions.

Proper management and communications training should be conducted at site and team meetings, including vendors, is a must at least once a week for smooth team management. A hands-on, fact-based approach like the one in the Indian Army is highly recommended for the FM.

A proper professional distance with clients, staff, and vendors should always be maintained. There should be no room for any loose talk on matters related to money or characters to be entertained at the site by the facilities manager at any level.

Also, proper whistleblowing and integrity breach report protocols should be followed by FM himself at all times.

Training on integrity workshops should be regular with all stakeholders, followed.

15

Generic Industry Constraints

FM industry has very low entry barriers for professionals, and a person from any background can enter. This creates a vast pool of resources with varied backgrounds. Secondly, very few formal courses and training modules are available for the general public, and the available ones are too costly and do not meet the needs of the average FM professional.

This has led to non-standard practices across the industry and a lack of understanding of the fundamentals.

Additionally, budget constraints and high stress of performance due to lower contract tenure, and TAT[1] for recruitment make the situation very challenging to find, recruit, and train the right resource in a short time as per client requirements.

Payment terms continue to be the biggest challenge for service providers, ranging anywhere from 30 to 120 days. This puts a huge financial burden on cash-strapped, low-margin business vendors, and is the main reason for poor quality of services and high staff turnover.

It is essential for the FM industry to acknowledge these concerns and to work out solutions, as it is they who are impacted and not clients. Only the ones who are progressive enough to achieve this will survive the worst economic scenario our country faces today post-COVID-19.

16

Vision for Post-Covid-19 FM Industry

COVID-19 has struck a huge blow on Indian and world economies. With restrictions on the number of staff working in offices for each organisation, there is immense pressure on real estate costs, and all expansion and recruitment plans of most companies are now indefinitely postponed. Manpower-based services will now face pressure and cuts. Here again, it can be treated as a huge opportunity to innovate internal processes by FMSPs and make them more efficient and cost-effective. The following initiatives are a must if survival is the target.

- Re-define each business process and critically evaluate manpower and technology requirements from a long-term cost reduction perspective.
- All unnecessary processes should be eliminated.
- Change of Business and Financial models to reduce overhead costs is a must now.
- Implementation of technology has no alternative now.

- Post-COVID, the economy has bounced back after and India is expected to grow exponentially as an alternative to China. A robust blueprint based on all the above parameters must be finalised and implemented at the earliest to reap the rewards when they come.

17

Conclusion

Despite industry and post-COVID constraints, this is the ideal time to improvise on old school of thought for management and financial processes in the Indian FM industry and become lean and mean to take advantage of the coming growth scenario.

This book is one such small step in this direction, with a conviction that when all constituents join forces, together we can achieve the impossible.

PART 2

Basics of Property Management in the Indian Context

Overview

With Global Corporate Offices, Warehouses, and Manufacturing Hubs coming to India in the twenty-first century, and now that India is ranking in the Top 5 Global Economies with a tag of the fastest-growing one, no other industry than the Real Estate Industry is in a better position to participate in this drive and reap the benefits of what can be called the "Indian Gold Rush" for the rest of the world.

Today, India has state-of-the-art commercial complexes, mini city-like commercial knowledge parks supporting specific industry segments such as infotech, biotech, chemical manufacturing, auto clusters, etc. With a global workforce moving to India from senior, mid to even managerial level staff, the boom for premium housing complexes has created a new specialised sector of residential property management.

However, it is in an infant stage to support Long-Term Asset Capitalisation Goals, and we have miles to go before we can take a deep breath and look back to measure our rate of growth.

Arguably, we are indeed building properties to global standards, be it LEED or GRESB. However, we still need to get into the mindset of maintaining the created assets at the same standard. This essentially involves end-user and maintenance agencies' education and training, which is the biggest challenge here.

The Global Market forces have now created corporate giants in the form of asset management companies, who hold the financial muscle to rule this market of commercial and residential spaces.

Co-working spaces are another reality putting margin pressures on a property management service provider.

In this section, we will cover the basics, best practices, and efficient business models of the future.

Basic Principal of Property Management

Maintenance Costs

-Cleaning

-MEP Maintenace

-Garbage Clearance

-Amenities

-Power Back up

-Water Charges

-Power Charges

-Govt Taxes & Duties

-Insurance/Fire Protection

Occupants-Direct Expenses

COMMON AREA MAINTENANCE (CAM)

Premises Maintenance Expenses

Property Management deals in managing the premises on behalf of builder/Owners Association. Whether it's a big residential complex or commercial building/township, we have occupiers who may be owners or lessees in the premises who stay and use the premises for personal or official purposes, and the premises have to be maintained according to the Laid down Municipal Bylaws and Labour Laws to ensure regular upkeep and maintenance. Key components can be:

- Building premises upkeep and maintenance
- Collection and Control of Maintenance Charges
- Emergency Management
- Occupant Wellbeing and Delightful Experience

Building over a Commercial Multitenant Complex

Good old days had big commercial complexes housing standard and non-standard offices with bare minimum shared amenities. Then, gradually, a flexi-model approach with a bare shell approach giving good flexibility to occupant lessees about what kind of basic inside infrastructure to choose - for example, the type of AC - window or split, etc.

This model worked well in the pre-globalisation era, where buildings were not so advanced and attractive, and were just complexes providing basic office setups and needs.

The Basic Mindset of Provision of Bare Minimum

The major challenge about infrastructure and in general planning of any amenity is the lack of budget, vision, or provision of common infrastructure. If there is no vision and budget, how can the essential common area infrastructures be built? So, whenever we see outdoor split AC units hanging out in balconies of commercial buildings or Water-dripping window ACs in corridors and walkways with a not-so-good-looking drain pipe and a makeshift collection bucket, it is still a very common sight inside well-known commercial buildings.

India needs to learn a lot from the Western world in planning and designing common area infrastructure, be it a high-end Airport, a standalone multi-tenant commercial building, or a residential complex.

Tips for Planning a Better Common Infrastructure

Here are a few brainstormers for the stakeholders to work on.

- If a Big Complex needs, say, 200 to 300 personnel to maintain the premises, they also require materials, spares, machines, etc., to work. Where are these people going to change/store material, have lunch, and repair machines?
- Where does the in-process inventory/scrap stored before it is processed out?

- Where should the essential critical stock of spares be stored properly so that it does not get damaged?
- Is the Size of the Property Management Office and Required Document Storage enough for the needs?
- Does the Building have aesthetic Grand areas like Podiums/Reception with Places/Lights at a Height of more than 20 feet? This would definitely require specialised cranes to clean and maintain after construction is over.

The Root cause of poor planning of above is lack of budget allocation. I am saying allocation of funds, not the funds itself, as this is where India is different than West or even China, for that matter. We should remember failing to plan is planning to fail, as these shortcomings in the Modern Building complexes result in poor and costly operating processes, guzzling the expenses out of CAM budget. Result of poor planning.

Better Plan, Better Build, Effective Management

Now that we have seen that Better Planning can save a lot of cost and troubles during the active building life in maintenance, it is always advisable to build efficient planning so that the Constructed Building will need very few alterations and adjustments in efficient maintaining.

Also, proper care should be taken in capability planning, especially where services like Air conditioning and STP are concerned. In huge complexes, enough design staging needs to be factored in to save on operating costs.

03

End-To-End PM Contract Management Cycle

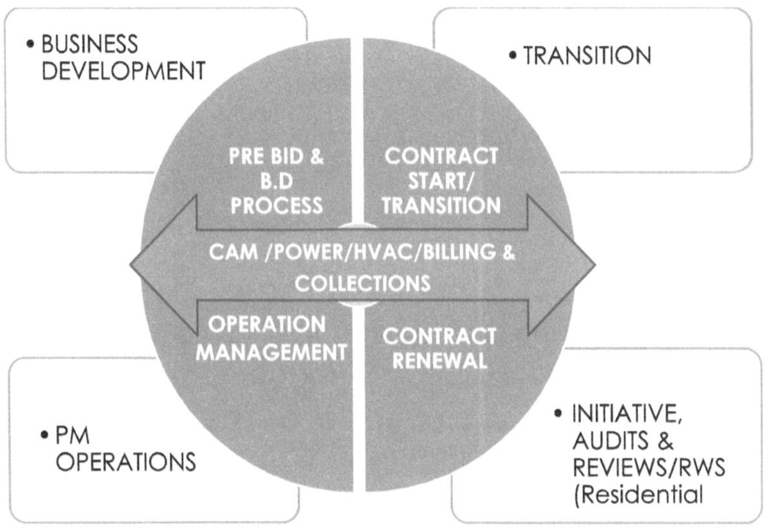

Business Development Stage: This stage usually begins 30 to 90 days before a contract is intended to start from the Client. Usually, there are 3 stages of any new business development or Bid stage as illustrated below. The first stage requires the Client to Prepare and circulate RFP document and organise visits and meetings for understanding of deliverables by Property Management Service Provider (PMSP).

The second stage consists of Compiling Proposals and evaluation of the best Service provider. The last stage is to award the contract.

Pre
- FLOATING OF RFP DOCUMENT TO VARIOUS PMSPs
- ORGANISING SITE VISITS AND PROVIDING THEM INFORMATION

Bid
- GETTING THE PROPOSALS FROM PMSPs
- ORGANISING PRESENTATION TO UNDERSTAND THE PROPOSAL
- EVALUATING COMPETENCY OF FMSP ON PROPOSAL AND ABILITY TO DELIVER SERVICES OF REQUIRED QUALITY

Post
- AWARD OF CONTRACT TO BEST QUALIFIED PMSP
- SIGNING OF CONTRACT AND COLLECTION OF RELEVANT BACK UP DOCUMENTS LIKE INSURANCES BG ETC

The Transition or Mobilisation Phase: The first 30 to 45-day period between contract awards and the startup of actual Property Management operations on the ground is referred to as the Transition or Mobilisation Phase. If the contract volume is large or consists of multiple sites or city operations, this phase may incur additional charges and would require extra resources or a separate transition team to ensure that the entire contract setup is completed and operations start on the due date. However, it is entirely a business decision between PMSP and the Client whether such services will be billed or included as value-added services from PMSP. The following are the various types of transition requirements.

- Transition of a New Site – Takeover from Projects, set up of FM operations, and Handover to Operations team
- Transition from Outgoing FMSP and takeover and setup of FM operations.
- Transition from in-house team to outsourced FMSP team and set up of operations.
- Finding out gaps or snags in the facility and assigning the cost, priority, and responsibility to it is also a major activity of transition.

Basically, it means capturing damages and costs that exist before the contract started. The client or outgoing project team/erstwhile PMSP should bear the rectification costs for these defects.

- The transition team is an important link to understand the awarded contract with scope and SLAs. It has to transfer this to the operations team through training induction and briefing as a part of the contract startup deliverable and take sign-off internally to ensure compliance.

Transition is a very critical phase of any Property Management contract, and the entire success or failure of the contract can be attributed to it. This is the reason that it is always preferable to have a separate Transition Team and Lead for every contract. The Transition team can be merged into the Operations team if required, providing flexibility to all parties. It is always advisable to form a skeletal transition team at the time of the Pre-Bid or Bid stage, and it is involved right from the RFP stage and the preparation of the proposal. It comes in handy, saves time, and increases the effectiveness of contract implementation when the contract is awarded.

However, the ready availability of a Transition team on the bench is very unlikely with any PMSP due to cost constraints. A good FMSP can be distinguished from the rest based on the ability to cater to this requirement in a short time within its resources without compromising the quality of the Transition.

Finding out and rectification of the Snags in Property and Infrastructure, the recruitment, on-site Training, and Deployment of Operations team, and Outsourced Vendors along with uniform, Tools, and Checklists, and standard control documentation are the most important deliverables of the Transition Phase. The expected SLA is above 95%, which will ensure the success of the contract accordingly.

Property Management - Operations Stage

PMSP has to ensure that above 90% of committed resources for the contract are available and deployed at the start date. Ideally, the on-site and on-job training, induction, and orientation have to be completed during the transition phase; however, practically, this should be completed within 15 days of the contract start date.

At the end of 35 days from the contract start date, PMSP is supposed to submit separately the Transitions and Monthly Operations report to the client, capturing all the operations and contractual obligation details.

In addition to the delivery of standard agreed SLAs, as per the contract, a PMSP is supposed to carry out internal audits as value-added services (Free of Cost) every quarter by engaging a In House or Third party Subject Matter Expert (SME). The services for internal audit are as listed below. The list is indicative and not exhaustive.

- Health & Safety Review
- Fire Evacuation Drills
- Soft Services Review
- Technical Audit
- Innovations and Process Improvements.
- Cost Saving and Benchmarking Initiatives

Successful implementation of the above will ensure the renewal of the contract and the longevity of a healthy client relationship.

Common Area Maintenance (CAM) Billing and Collections

Refer to the diagram on page 33 and 65. If we compare this with the facility Management Operations and Business Cycle, we can spot the arrow mentioning "CAM Billing and Collections", which appears in the Property Management Life Cycle but is not present in the FMSP Business Process.

Let's understand it further. The Common Areas maintenance charges, referred to as CAM charges, are the expenses accrued in maintaining the Common Areas of Building Premises. The Common Areas mainly consist of:

- Lift Lobbies, Atrium, Building Common Reception
- Parking Areas, Common Basements, Driveways
- Shared manned and other services like premises security, cleaning, pest control, horticulture, fountains, and Water bodies, etc.
- Staircases, Terraces, Common Canteens, Food Courts, Sports, Gym Facilities.
- Essential Services such as Lifts, Fire Fighting Systems, Lighting, Electrical Power Distribution, Plumbing, Sewage Treatment, Drainage, and HVAC Infrastructure for Building Common Areas.

The expenses accrued for providing and maintaining the entire premises due to the above points are recovered or billed to all occupants based on the area they occupy and proportionately divided among them.

In addition, in Centralised Air-conditioned buildings, the HVAC, the Water, and in many cases, the electrical power required by the respective occupant are provided directly by the premise owner (builder), and the same is metered and billed as per prevalent rates of these utilities.

HVAC Charges - These are metered using BTU Metres (which stands for 'British Thermal Units', wherein 1 tonne is equal to 12,000 BTU), capturing the power consumed by the respective occupant in KWH.

Illustration*

A building with a total leasable area of 1 million square feet has the following monthly expenses recorded:

1. Security Services – INR 300,000
2. Cleaning Services – INR 250,000
3. Technical Maintenance Team charges – INR 200,000
4. Pest Control – INR 5000
5. Horticulture – INR 50,000
6. Repairs & Maintenance, Including Equipment Maintenance Contract Charges – INR 2,000,000
7. Water Charges – INR 300,000
   Tenants Power Metered Total, INR 2,000,000
   Total Power Cost for Premises: INR 3,500,000
8. Common Area Power Cost* - INR 1,500,000 (Difference between Total Power Cost and tenants' Total Power Cost).
9. Common Area HVAC - INR 500,000
10. Thus Total Maintenance Cost for month is Total of all expenses above- INR 51,05,000.00

This would translate to INR 5.105 per square foot, CAM charges (Common Area Maintenance) for the month.

Please refer to the table for details. Normally, at the design stage for the premises, the CAM charges are pre-calculated at full occupancy and load of the building and are part of the lease agreement as a fixed cost per square foot. Amount billed per month.

Table for Illustration

S No	Type	Head	Amount
1	Manpower	Security	300000
2	Manpower	Cleaning	250000
3	Manpower	MEP Team	200000
4	Manpower	Horticulture	50000
5	R&M	Pest Control	5000
6	R&M	Repairs & maintenance,	2000000
7	Utility	Water charges	300000
8	Utility	Common Area Electricity,	1500000
9	Utility	Common Area BTU, HVAC	500000
		Total Cam Recoverable Amount	51050000
		Building CAM Cost, INR/Sqft	**5.105**

Thus, every month, the Common Area Maintenance charges reconciliation is done when Utility Bills are Received, and respective occupants are billed each month over and above lease rental charges. The Property Management PMSP cost is also added to the CAM charges.

Other non-billable costs to the occupants are the capital expenditures incurred by the property owner and expenses incurred in building certification and registration.

Quality of Service Delivery, Service Delivery

The Quality of Buildings is now measured by the certifications they have for construction and operation. Energy Efficiency and Overall Maintenance standards indicate the Building's Global rating. The most common modern rating system includes LEED (Leadership in Energy and Environmental Efficient Design) certification, which indicates energy efficiency. The rating varies from Silver, Gold, to Platinum based on design and operating models for energy efficiency.

LEED certification ensures energy efficiency, productivity, and profitability of all occupants based on efficient design.

GRESB standards are now followed based on the carbon footprint it leaves and the green parameters.

In addition, the Quality Health & Safety Standards designed and adhered to are measured by IMS/BSC standards, which are a must now for any building or property of large scale.

In turn, it increases premiums for rentals and sales and is sought after by most of the leading occupants worldwide.

Clients usually review the performance of PMSP every month and on a quarterly basis at senior management levels based on predefined Key Performance Indicators (KPIs), which link a portion of the Property Management Fee as a penalty in case of non-achievement of set KPIs.

Contract Renewal Stage: This may be a repeat of the entire Bid Process or simply a commercial renegotiation depending on PMSP Performance and Client Requirements. In case the contract is not renewed or is lost, PMSP is required to **Demobilise** the site, which is kind of the reverse or opposite of mobilisation or Transition. Here, the PMSP has to close the operations and relocate its staff in accordance with the Contract and Client requirements.

Resident Welfare Association

The Property Management can be classified based on the Type of Client portfolio into 2 main segments, namely residential and commercial. The residential sector deals with large residential complexes. The Operating Principle here is that the builder constructs housing complexes under RERA legislation. Then, according to the law, once the property is ready and the Occupation Certificate (OC) is issued by the Local Municipal Body, the Developer has to hand over the Maintenance of the Property to the Residents' Committee, called the Resident Welfare Association or Society (RWS).

Usually, the Committee has to be formed within 90 days of OC and Registration/Occupation; however, by the time the residents occupy the premises, hold an election, and form the RWS, it usually takes anywhere between 1 to 3 years. This is a critical period where technically the Developer maintains the premises and uses the funds collected in the RWS account under maintenance expenses as per RERA rules. Usually, the Developer always provisions expenses up to a year for this activity to maintain continuity of PM operations on-site.

All major developers nowadays appoint a PMSP on their behalf during this period to maintain premises. In such a case, when the RWS is ready to take over, the PMSP may have to participate in a fresh RFP or tender process organised by RWS and compete with other agencies to retain the PMS contract.

This is also one of the main differentiators between Facilities and Property Management Services.

Technical Services

Maintenance of Electrical Infrastructure

Typically, a property, whether residential or commercial, has either a High Tension (11KV) connection from the power supply company or a Low Tension (400V) connection. In the case of an HT connection, transformers are used to step down the voltage, and a switchyard (ref. pic) is part of the property. The power distribution is done through a substation that houses power panels.

First is the provision of qualified, licensed, and trained manpower for Operation & Maintenance (O&M), along with necessary tools and tackles as required.

The main activities:

- Deputing HT/LT Electrical Licence-Holding Supervisor and Engineering Staff.
- Daily Collecting Readings of Energy Metres for Power Consumption, Data, and Sharing with Property Management Team for Further Client Billing and Records.
- Daily/weekly/monthly/quarterly maintenance and checks of operating electrical equipment - lights and power as per "**Planned Preventive Maintenance**."
- **Schedule,** popularly known as **PPM schedule**,
- Ensuring 100% uptime of all electrical and power backup equipment like D G Set UPS, etc..
- Ensuring proper Quality of Electrical Power (Voltage/Current/Earthing/Phase Balanced).

Electro-Mechanical and HVAC

Mechanical systems in properties are mainly:

- Ventilation Fans: Used for parking, toilet, and Staircase exhaust (in case of fire)
- Lifts and escalators.

Picture 1: Lifts in Commercial Buildings

Picture 2: Facade Glass Cleaning System

- Specialised Systems, Such as Facade Glass Cleaning System

Picture 3: Hydro-pneumatic Water Supply Pumps

- – Pumps: Water Supply and Sewage Pumping.
- – HVAC or Air conditioning systems.

Provision of qualified and trained manpower for operating and maintaining mechanical systems, including pumps, chiller plants, Air conditioning system compressors, etc.

Types of HVAC Systems

Typically, big commercial complexes have chiller plants, Water or Air Cooled, and big IT Parks may have a Central District Cooling Plant.

Picture 4: HVAC Chiller Plant

Picture 5: HVAC Cooling Towers

HVAC system is the largest component of power consumption in any commercial complex. Hence, it is very important for the PM team to ensure the system is run in an efficient manner by maintaining proper set points of chillers and proper scheduling of various equipment like cooling towers, pumps, Air handling units, and chilled Water balancing, etc.

Plumbing, Water Supply and Drainage/ Sewage System

An efficient plumbing system includes proper capacity design of Water Tanks, Pumping System and the Piping Network. High-Rise buildings have multiple Pressure-Reducing Valves on each floor, and special care has to be taken to ensure proper access is available to reach and service all critical components. Usually, it is observed that pipes supplying Water and carrying sewage down are housed in small shafts that are difficult to access and not supportive of any maintenance activity carried out. Like any other system, the plumbing system ages faster and frequently breaks down with a huge impact due to leakage, etc., because of non-serviceability of critical assets owing to access issues.

While all modern commercial and residential complexes have a Sewage Treatment Plant (STP) that ensures wastewater is recycled, the major issue is the sizing of the STP. Big STPs for big complexes take time to be usable until the load reaches 40 to 50% of capacity. This results in challenges during the initial occupancy phase, which may range from a couple of months to a couple of years. A properly planned alternative approach is essential to mitigate this health and safety issue.

One more caution that needs to be taken is that all main supply lines and outlets need to have robust metres, which should be designed to be installed and replaced without impacting services.

Civil Structure Maintenance and Painting

Proper Loading Details for Slabs and Drawings Pertaining to Structures are a very important part of Property Management.

A ready reckoner of Loading Chart and other structural details should be handy with the PM team responsible for fit-out.

The facade design and paints used in the structure also need to be maintained by the civil team.

Fit-Out Management:

Usually, all Leased Spaces available in commercial complexes or residential Societies are Bare Shell, with only utilities like Water, and Power/LPG/ HVAC/Fire Connection points available for a new occupant.

Fire safety systems - Hydrants, Sprinklers, Vesda, Alarm Systems.

Lighting and Electrical Power Distribution Systems.

Security System: CCTV, Access Control, Boom Barriers.

Building Management System (BMS)

Services Delivery Methodology

Any client requiring the provision of hard services issues a "Request for Proposal" or RFP to the interested FM Service Providers or MEP contractors. The client may also ask Project Management or Installation of Systems companies to quote for hard services when starting a new facility. An RFP contains a brief overview.

- The Make, Quantity, Type, and Specifications of MEPC installations.
- List of all Assets with warranty details.
- Operating hours and specific manpower requirements (qualification/experience, etc.).
- Type of Maintenance required: Comprehensive and Non-Comprehensive.
- Quality of outputs or service levels expected are also specified.

Usually, a site visit is also organised for interested parties, where they are expected to conduct a detailed survey and ask questions for a better understanding of client requirements, and to determine the manpower, materials, and tools required to perform the activities for the desired client output.

All Proposals and Costs are then requested and sought by the client in a typical format. Usually, the proposals are sought for a manpower cost-plus basis. The proposals are per month manpower deployed costs for a period of a minimum 12-month contract period, up to many more years' extendable contract.

Service Delivery Procedure

1. Asset List and PPM Schedule finalised and approved.
2. Opex and Capex budgets made and approved.
3. Tools, Spares, and Consumables ordered and stocked.
4. Checklists/Log books and History Cards for all Equipment are made.
5. SOPs, safety documents like risk assessment, and work permits are made available on the ground.
6. Basic Induction and training to all Staff and Vendors.
7. Outsourced Services Contracts and SLAs agreed and implemented.
8. Daily/Weekly/Monthly reports of Corrective and Preventive maintenance are maintained on CAFM or manually as per the Contract.
9. Asset and Service Health Status is reported in MMR and Reviewed.
10. Regular Service/Tool/Quality, and Safety Audits as per client SOP.

04

Soft Services

These are mainly non-technical services listed as below.

- Cleaning Services
- Waste Management
- Horticulture
- Pest Control
- Security and Guarding
- Pantry and Cafeteria Services Management

These are usually manpower and service output requirement-based services.

Service Delivery Methodology

Here, the client usually floats an RFP, followed by a site survey visit to understand the scope of services and then works out the manpower, tools, and material requirements for the desired level of output.

All Proposals and Costs are then requested and sought by the client in a typical format. Usually, the proposals are sought for a manpower cost-plus basis. The proposals are per month manpower deployed costs for a period of a minimum 12-month contract period, up to many more years' extendable contract.

Service Delivery Procedure

The Procedure for Service Delivery is similar to hard services. A summary, for easy understanding, is as follows:

Service	Scope of Work	Daily	Weekly	Fortnightly	Monthly	Quarterly	Half Yearly	Annual	MIS	Monitoring Measure
Cleaning	√	Activity/Deliverable SLA							Available	Performance Control
Waste Management	√	Activity/Deliverable SLA							Available	Performance Control
Horticulture	√	Activity/Deliverable SLA							Available	Performance Control
Pest Control	√	Activity/Deliverable SLA							Available	Performance Control
Security & Guarding	√	Activity/Deliverable SLA							Available	Performance Control
Pantry Sevices	√	Activity/Deliverable SLA							Available	Performance Control
Cafetaria Management	√	Activity/Deliverable SLA							Available	Performance Control

1. Area Cleaning Schedule finalised and approved
2. Opex and Capex budget made and approved.
3. Tools, Spares, and Consumables Ordered and Stocked
4. Checklists/Log books for all activities and areas are made.
5. SOPs, Safety Documents like Risk Assessment, and Work Permits are made available on the ground.
6. Basic Induction and training to all Staff and Vendors.

7. Outsourced Services Contracts, such as Carpet Shampooing, Glass Cleaning, etc., and SLAs agreed and implemented.
8. Daily/Weekly /Monthly reports of Corrective and Regular maintenance are maintained on CAFM or manual as per Contract.
9. Cleaning Status is reported in MMR and Reviewed.
10. Regular Service/Tool/Quality, and Safety Audits as per client SOP

05

General Admin Support Services

These are the office support services that most of the clients nowadays prefer to outsource to minimise their on-roll staff requirement, giving them flexibility and reducing overhead costs. The main interest is to increase the output of these services without creating a liability for the client organisation. Typical admin support services are as listed.

- Reception and Front Desk
- Event Management
- Reprographic stations management
- Stationery and office Supplies Management
- Helpdesk
- Documents and records management
- Asset Furniture and Fixture Management

As a general guideline, the following are important points to be considered:

1. A Sound Policy for all above services, well defined and communicated to all users.
2. In case of software-based management, proper training and a back-end contract with the supplier should be ensured.

3. Proper Storage Place - Online and Offline to be made available
4. Procurement and Billing Interfaces clearly understood and communicated to all team.
5. Proper JD to be made, and training at regular intervals is a must.

06

Specialist Services

These are the specialised systems related maintenance services which may require an expert to maintain them. However, usually, these services are designed to be maintained by periodic inspections and, as and when required, visits by the Original Equipment Manufacturers' representative only, who is authorised to carry out the maintenance jobs.

The operations of these systems can be carried out by the regular on-site maintenance team, but they must be trained by the OEM representative on a regular basis. The following is a list of such services or systems, which is indicative only.

- Audio Visual Systems
- Facade Cleaning and Maintenance
- Fire Systems Maintenance
- Computer server-related special CRAC Aircon units.
- UPS systems
- Building Management Systems
- Parking Management System
- Lifts, elevators, and escalators

- Security Systems, such as CCTV, Access Control, FAS.
- Diesel Gensets
- Chillers
- Water Pumping Systems
- Space and Move Management
- Staff Transport Services - Pick up and Drop
- Concierge and Travel Desk Management

Cost-Plus or All-Inclusive option

Usually, all these costs are directly paid by the clients, and FMSP is supposed to only coordinate for service delivery. However, now in many cases, the client may ask for these services to be maintained and billed by FMSP. **However, as the assets here belong to the client, it is always recommended that these services are maintained and paid for directly by the client.**

07

Quality, Health & Safety

This subject has become of utmost importance in the modern age due to increased awareness and costs associated with quality and health & safety of staff within any premises, be it commercial or residential property.

The main objective in the QHSE field for any organisation is to clearly spell out the policy document and ensure that each staff and vendor working on its premises is aware of it. This awareness needs to be translated into training and knowledge to ensure that safety rules and guidelines are followed in all aspects of work at all times, and proper records are maintained for legal purposes in the future.

Important Deliverables of QHSE Policy Document

- Risk identification and Mitigation, Risk Register.
- First Aid Provision Maintenance
- Incidents, Near Misses, Accident Investigation, and Records
- Emergency Evacuation Plan and readiness
- Fire Safety Drill Calendar

- List of Fire Wardens
- Safety Jackets, Masks, Torches, etc., for Wardens
- Power Backup Parameters, Testing Procedures, and dates.
- Statutory Compliances, Inspections, and Dates, Technical and Non-technical
- PQA, Indoor Air, and Water, Food Quality Test dates.
- OSHA guidelines
- Site Safety Manual
- Work Permits, PTW, Working at Height/Confined spaces, critical infrastructure.

08

Compliances Management

All the services, whether technical or non-technical, are governed by Shops and Establishment, Minimum Wages, and other Labour acts. It is the responsibility of the client as a principal employer to ensure compliance. The client usually, in the contract to FMSP, puts the responsibility of compliance on the facility manager. The following are the most important compliances that must be maintained on-site at all times and can be inspected by a Labour inspector or competent authority at any time.

- Attendance and Wage Register for all contract staff at the site.
- Adherence to provisions of the Contract Labour Registration Act (CLRA), including, but not limited to, PF and ESIC challans, paid copies.
- In case of Transport management – Vehicle Compliances, Driver Compliances, and Tax Paid receipts.
- Test Certificates for Water Tanks, Foods, Air Quality, and D.S. Sets Returns.

- Annual Electrical, Fire and Lift Inspections by Statutory Authorities.
- Consent to Operate (CTO), PWD, and Municipality Inspections for sanitation and hygiene.
- Pest Control Records
- Penal Deduction records for SLA-related contracts
- Payment Certificates to all Contractors.
- Facade Cleaning, Inspection, and Test Certificates
- Payment of Govt. Taxes and Duties, as applicable, such as Annual Fire and Lift Inspections, property Tax, etc.

09

Introduction to Property Management Software

PM Software has become an essential part of any PM Contract, be it residential or commercial. Usually, it means a specialised, generic or specific software tool either provided by the Client or in FMSP scope with the following essential features.

- A Complaint Management Module (CMMS) to record, track, and evaluate the customer service requests and generate MIS with accurate analysis on SLAs in each category of Service.
- A PPM module for tracking the effectiveness of preventive maintenance of assets.
- A Financial module to assist in capturing Common Area Maintenance costs, expenses, and tracking the budget of various categories of services.
- Visitor Management System for Assisting security in safe access to premises for staff, vendors, and visitors.
- Parking management system for parking, management

- Time and Attendance monitoring,
- Automated, QR code-based, and geo-fencing-based Quality of Services monitoring
- MIS module for Daily, Weekly, Monthly, and other specific reports, as required by the Contract, along with the capability to store scanned service reports of Outsourced vendors or specialist suppliers.

This software may be paid on actuals by the client or may be included in contract costs, depending on the contract and client requirements. Care has to be taken to include or cover its costs in the proposal by PMSP and should not be missed out by any chance.

Usually, help desk executives are expected to manage the software. However, access to different teams for different modules is given based on actual need.

A range of high-end to local software (like Maximo from IBM) is available in the market, and many clients and PMSPs have developed their own software.

However, like the FM industry, even property management Software is often poorly implemented across the industry due to ambiguity, lack of clarity, authority, cost, and bureaucratic delays between the client, PMSP, and vendors. It is therefore very important for all parties to understand the importance of its implementation. Non-implementation and delays

often lead to wasted time and efforts by all parties at all management levels, affecting the quality of services and customer satisfaction.

App-based Mobility Solutions for technical teams checking the assets are also very common. However, such a requirement has to be studied in detail before any cost commitment is made or sought from any party as it is very costly to implement and does not have the flexibility for FMSP to absorb costs in case of poor implementation or failure.

Final Note From the Author

In this book we have tried to cover the basics of property and facility management industry in India. We hope that this book has provided sufficient details on basic requirements from a client and Service Provider's perspective for a beginner in this industry.

Our Armed Forces - Army, Navy and Air Force contribute a lot in terms of providing alternative employment to personnel retiring after Short and Long Service Commissions in Property and Facility Management Industry. Especially for Non Commissioned or JCO or Sepoy/Soldier/Engineer Rank personnel, this book will help to orient them into civilian PFM world by priming them with basic information as required.

This book is a small step in trying to give back to the industry which has built the career of the author with lots of gratitude and love.

Noted Recommendations

Appendices

- Annexure-1 - Daily Service call Report Format
- Annexure-2 - MOM Format
- Annexure-3 - Snag list Format
- Annexure-4 - Transition Tracker Format
- Annexure-5 - Transition Report Format
- Annexure-6 - MMR Format
- Annexure-7 - Weekly Roster Format
- Annexure-8 - Critical Infrastructure Checklist
- Annexure-9 - Audit review Format
- Annexure-10 - QBR (Quarterly Business Review) Format
- Annexure-11 - SLA Report Format
- Annexure-12 - Weekly Report Format
- Annexure-13 - Operations Tracker Format
- Annexure-14 - Suppliers AMC Tracker

Daily Service call Report Format

Date	

#	Service	Priority	Received Calls	Pending calls	Status	Remarks
1	Aircon	P 1	3	0		Closed within TAT
2	Plumbing	P 2	2	0		Closed within TAT
3	Electrical	P 3	1	0		Closed within TAT
4	Mechanical	P 4	0	0		Closed within TAT
5	Carpentary	P 5	1	1		Closed within TAT
6	Housekeeping	P 2	5	0		Closed within TAT
7	Pest Control	P 3	0	0		Closed within TAT
8	General	P 4	2	1		Closed within TAT
9	Soft Services-General	P 2	1	0		Closed within TAT
10	Misclaneous	P 1	3	0		Closed within TAT
11	Others	P 2	2	0		Closed within TAT
	Total		**20**	**2**		

Daily Service call Report Format

Priority	Type	Description	Response Time	Resolution Time	Illustrations	Follow up
P1	Critical	Impacting Health & Safety Of Staff or Impacting Business or Both	within 15 Minutes	within 2 to 4 hours	Power Failure, Earthquake, Fire Emergency, Terror Threat, Accident/ Spillage of Harmful Chemical, Gas Leak etc	Usually attended by Specially Trained Staff / Emergency Response team (ERT) or Qualified Trained Staff such as Technicians /engineers
P2	Urgent	Will Impact Business or HSE if not done immidietly	2 to 4 hours	within 24 hours	Breakdown in Power/Water Supply, Waste extraction	Usually such cases are covered with Maintenance Agencies in Annual Contracts and critical spares are kept stored at Location for quick resolution
P3	Important	Potential to Impact Business or HSE if not planned and attended on priority	Same day	Within a week	Overheating in Electrical Circuit or Noisy Pump or jerking elevator etc	Cost Estimate to be ready and approved in 2 days and work executed within 3 days -overall One Business week

Priority	Type	Description	Response Time	Resolution Time	Illustrations	Follow up
P4	Normal	No Business Impact , Good to Have	2 to 4 days	within 2 to 4 weeks	Parking Request, Event Request etc	To Increase Customer Satisfaction
P5	General	No Business Impact , request by user	within a week	as per mutual convinience	Value additions for the Standards of existing processes	Feel Good Customer Touch points
P6	Specific/ Typical	Calls for Change in Design or Process Modification to increase effectiveness or effiency of Business and People	As per Specific need	Defined by Specific task	Involving capital Expenditure or Special Permission may involve shutdown maintenance or Planned Business outage without Business Impact	Technological Improvements, Automation, Audit or Survey etc

MOM Format

MINUTES OF MEETING

Date	
Present	
Company A	(Names)
Company B	(Names)

#	Discussed as	Action by	Target date	Actual Date	Status	Remarks

Snag List Format

S No	Site	Service	Location	Sub Location	Observation	Photo	Priority	Cost Estimate	Action By	Target Date	Actual Date	Status	Remarks
1	Site 1	HVAC	4th Floor East Wing	Unit 401	Air Handling Unit electrical connection pending		P1	N A	HVAC Contractor				

Transition Tracker Format

S No	Department	Activity	Schedule Date	Actual Date	Action By	Status	Remarks
1	Business Developemnt	Collect LOI/Contract fromClient					
2	Operations	Sending List of Positions to HR					
3	HR	Identify Existing Resources for New Project					
4	Operations	Deploy Existing Resources					
5	Operations	Interview and Hire New Resources					
6	IT	Issue of Laptop and Uniform to new staff					
7	Procurement	Hiring of Vendors					
8	Procurement	Purchase of Consumables, Tools , Machines and Spares					
9	Operations	Creating Site Office, Stores etc					
10	Operations	Site Mobilisation					
11	Operations	Take Over from Project Team					
12	Operations	Commecing PM Operations at Site					
13	Finance	Billing for Services					
14	Operations	Submission of Transition Report to Client					

Transition Report Format

Not Started   In Progress   Finished

S No	Site	Process	Activity	Status	Action By	Target Date	Actual Date	Status	Remarks
1	Site 1	**Legal**	Contract Issue						Contract Signing in Process
2	Site 1	**Transition Start**	Deployment of Transition Team						
			Hiring of resources						
			Hiring of Vendors						
			Site Mobilisation						
3	Site 1	**MEPC**	**Commisioning Witness and Services Takeover for**						
			HVAC						
			Plumbing						
			Electrical						
			Fire						

4	Site 1	**Transition Closure**	Admin						
			Civil						
			Safety						
			Training						
			Snaglist Update						
			Operations Team Deployment and Training, Takeover with Keys and office						
			Site Mobilisation						
			SOPs, Reporting and Billing Finalisation						
			Submission of MMR and Review Meet						
			Transition Closure Report						

Typical MMR Contents Format

1. **Contents**

2. **Occupancy Analysis & Fitout Tracker**

3. **Manpower Deployment Analysis**

4. **Equipment Downtime Tracker**

5. **PPM & AMC Tracker**

6. **Helpdesk Complaints & Leakage Tracker Analysis**

7. **Energy Consumption –Power/Water Consumption for Month**

8. **Sewage Water**

9. **Waste Management**

10. **Training Details**

11. **Major Achievements**

12. **Major issues**

Weekly Roster Format

Name	Designation	01-Apr	02-Apr	03-Apr	04-Apr	05-Apr	06-Apr	07-Apr
		Mon	Tue	Wed	Thu	Fri	Sat	Sun
Technical Team								
Mahesh	Shift Engineer	A	A	A	A	A	B	Off
Suresh	Shift Engineer	B	B	B	B	Off	C	C
Akhilesh	Shift Engineer	C	C	C	Off	B	A	A
Govind	Shift Engineer	G	G	G	G	C	Off	B
Lakshmi	Helpdesk	G	G	G	G	G	G	Off
Saraswati	Executive	G	G	G	G	G	G	Off
Housekeeping Team								
Shyam	Executive	A	A	A	A	A	B	Off
Ram	Executive	B	B	B	B	Off	C	C
Jhamu	Executive	C	C	C	Off	B	A	A
Santosh	Executive	G	G	G	G	C	Off	B
Vineet	A Manager	G	G	G	G	G	G	Off
Surkha	Manager	G	G	G	G	G	G	Off

Critical Infra CL Format

Infrastructure	Jan-25	Feb-25	Mar-25	Apr-25	May-25	Jun-25	Jul-25	Aug-25	Sep-25
Backup Power-DG	100%	100%	100%	100%	100%	100%	100%	100%	68%
Backup Power-UPS	100%	100%	100%	100%	100%	100%	100%	100%	100%
Fire Systems	100%	100%	100%	100%	100%	100%	100%	100%	100%
Server Room Acs	99%	94%	90%	90%	92%	98%	97%	97%	99%
Domestic Supply and Water Pumps	100%	98%	76%	76%	75%	76%	76%	76%	76%
HVAC Plant	100%	76%	100%	100%	100%	100%	100%	100%	100%
Lifts	98%	100%	95%	92%	95%	100%	99%	100%	98%
STP and Pumps	75%	75%	75%	75%	75%	75%	75%	75%	75%
Overall Uptime	**99%**	**93%**	**91%**	**90%**	**92%**	**95%**	**94%**	**94%**	**93%**

Audit Review Format

Sr. No.	Audit Description	Agency Name	Total Points	Closed Points	Open Points	% Closure
1	Fire Systems					-
2	Lift Audit					-
3	Energy Audit					-
4	Water Audit					-
5	HSE Audit					-
6	Soft Services Audit					
7	Technical Process Audit					-
8	Structural Audit					-
9	Labour Compliance Audit					-
10	Municipal Audit					-
11	Lift Inspection					
12	Electrical Inspection					
	Total					-

QBR (Quarterly Business Review) Format

SR. No.	Index Table
1	MOM of Previous Meeting
2	New Team Additions
3	Occupancy / Fitout Report
4	Customer Experience Insight
5	Helpdesk Performance Review
6	Power, Water Consumption Data
7	Equipment Uptime Statistics
8	Audit & Compliance Score Overview
9	Soft Services
10	Waste Management
11	EHS Report
12	Budget Vs Actual
13	Highlights
14	Challenges
15	Plan for Next Quarter

SLA Report Format

Sr. No.	Service	SLA	Penalty	Reward	Remarks
1	Critical Infrastructure	99% Uptime. Not More than 1 Failure	Rs 10000 per Incident owing to Negligence of Team		Deduction from M fee
2	Security Services	Audit Per Quarter, No Incident	Rs 10000 per Incident owing to Negligence of Team		Deduction from M fee
3	Housekeeping	Not More than 1 Incident			Deduction from M fee
4	Horticulture	99%			Deduction from M fee
5	Pest Control	No Schedule Missed			Deduction from M fee
6	Waste Management	95% Recycling			Deduction from M fee
7	Technical Services				Deduction from M fee
8	AMC Services	No Schedule Missed			Deduction from M fee
9	Customer Escalations		1000 per		Deduction from M fee
10	Budget Achievement	100% Adherence			Deduction from M fee
11	Innovations			5000 Per	
12	Appreciations Received				

118

Weekly Report Format

S No	Dept	Planned Activities	Status	Remarks

Operations Tracker Format

S No	Dept	Project	Dept	Task	Action by	Target Date	Status	Actual Date	Remarks
1	HR	OIC	MEP	Hiring of Shift Engineer					
2	HR	OIC	MEP	Hiring of Technical Manager					
3	HR	OWC	MEP	Hiring of Shift Engineer					
4	HR	OIC	All DRs and Team	Goal Setting					

AMC Tracker Format

#	Equipment	System	Supplier	Frequency	Type of AMC	Valid From	Valid Till	Remarks
1	Baggage Scanner	Security Sytems			CAMC	01-Apr-22	31-Mar-25	
2	CCTV	Security Sytems			NCAMC	01-Apr-22	31-Mar-25	
3	Access Controls	Security Sytems			CAMC	01-Apr-22	31-Mar-25	
4	Chillers-High Side	HVAC			Services	01-Apr-22	31-Mar-25	
5	Low Side	HVAC			CAMC	01-Apr-22	31-Mar-25	
6	Panels & Switchgear	Electrical			Services	01-Jul-22	31-Mar-25	
7	UPS	Power Back up			NCAMC	01-Apr-22	31-Mar-25	
8	DG	Power Back up			NCAMC	01-Apr-24	31-Mar-25	

About the Author

The Author is a Technocrat and Seasoned Professional with over 31 Years of Professional work experience in similar fields with exposure to Indian and Middle East Markets. He has been in the field of Property and Facilities management since 1999 and has hands-on experience in handling varied assignments ranging from Residential to Diverse Commercial Complexes, IT/ITES, BPO/KPO industries and allied service industry of Transport, Records Management, Events etc.